In a lyric collection of profound beauty and grief,
This Is How the Bone Sings by W. Todd Kaneko carries the
pulse of ancient lament through the boneyards of war
and unspeakable trauma. Kaneko's powerful songs of
ancestral fatherhood illuminate the haunting melancholia
of exile and internment: "When I dream, I see an open
meadow / from my father's living room / windows, the
house drained of color / except for the dissolve of night,
/ a splash of fire, an angel's mane / untamed for the first
time / since suffering a gash of spurs." The graceful poems
hover in the air like elusive promises of hope overshad-
owed by heartache, loss, and betrayal persisting long after
a time of war: "We believe not in ghosts but in flowers,
/ in the shape of a blossom that appears / every spring
and whispers that word / our family uses in the place of
ghosts." In a world at once beautiful and grotesque, the
poet must "hew an orchard out of the night" as a space
of survival. *This Is How the Bone Sings* reminds us to share
our tales of generational trauma and topography—
shaping our individual and collective memories—in place
of forgotten histories. —KAREN AN-HWEI LEE,
Author of *Phyla of Joy* and *The Maze of Transparencies*

The best books about history are those that are also about
the future. W. Todd Kaneko's marvelous This is How
the Bone Sings is more than a mere song—it is a singing
across time and distance. In lyrics both personal and
political, Kaneko composes a score that spans four gener-
ations, connecting his grandparents, who were prisoners
in the unfathomable Minidoka concentration camps, to
his young son and this unfathomable era in which he was
born. One of the many things I love about this book is

Kaneko's willingness to ask big questions: what lessons about the present can we learn from the past? What is the inheritance of trauma? Can anything not be repeated? Ultimately, though, it is the craft of these poems that converts the experiences of history into the experience of art. This is a must read. —DEAN RADER, Author of *Self Portrait as Wikipedia Entry*

To enter this book is to enter an orchard alive with memory's beasts. To read *This Is How the Bone Sings* is to witness how a poet at the height of his powers can alchemize history's violence into lyric and myth. W. Todd Kaneko's gutting and transformative collection begins in Minidoka, the site of his family's incarceration, and travels far beyond it: to lands where ogres roam, where witches wander midnight trees, where a grandmother's ghost haunts an arrow-shadowed house. As yonsei (fourth generation Japanese American) poets, we wonder often—to ourselves, to each other—how to respond to our children's "carnivorous question": Where is Minidoka? Minidoka: site of survival and confinement, the place where our country practiced "how to kill people / without killing them," the desert prison where "our families learned to be beasts." Minidoka: our collective nightmare, our ghosts' shared dream. *This Is How the Bone Sings* returns me to the deep ancestral howl crying out from our communal histories; it also returns me to my humanity. —BRYNN SAITO, Author of *Power Made Us Swoon*

In Kaneko's highly-anticipated *This Is How the Bone Sings*, we are introduced to characters mythical and marvelous in landscapes where "...hands can be stealthy, lovesick foxes or tiny owls who doubt the night." These are much-needed poems of unapologetic tenderness and talent—in other words, this collection does the near-impossible: it points us towards love even if what we know of this world doesn't. —AIMEE NEZHUKUMATATHIL, Author of *Oceanic* and *Lucky Fish*

What does it mean to be safe in America? In *This Is How the Bone Sings*, W. Todd Kaneko explores the legacy of concentration camps in the United States and how memory is carried forward. Brilliant and inventive in its use of form, Kaneko weaves in haikus as sentences and haibun as reading comprehension quizzes. Reaching into myth and ancestry, these poems pull out rich narratives and lyricism, where even in the most brutal pasts, horses whisper truths and a boy is born of a peach. Kaneko interrogates a nation with its own language and with places it has almost erased. This book knows how to sing—to America, not its expected script, but the anthems of its history; and to a son, lessons on how to bring back the dead with stories, with a fading map, with birds. —TRACI BRIMHALL, Author of *Come the Slumberless to the Land of Nod*

THIS IS HOW THE
BONE SINGS

Poems by W. Todd Kaneko

**Black
Lawrence
Press**

www.blacklawrence.com

Executive Editor: Diane Goettel
Cover Design: "Remembering Minidoka" by W. Todd Kaneko
Book Design: Zoe Norvell

Copyright © W. Todd Kaneko 2020
ISBN: 978-1-62557-133-5

Published 2020 by Black Lawrence Press.

for Leo and the twins

TABLE OF CONTENTS

WHERE WE LIVE NOW

SILENCE

the birds know what they mean

The birds say, Minidoka—
what I mean is that the juniper
is full of life in December,

hardy sparrows, oblivious
to stories about birds
who lose their tongues.

They mean that we can remain
invisible, as if a ragged tree
could be an icebox,
as if it could hold every bird

in America. A man can speak
about history, as if orchards
have never been tangled

in barbed wire, as if a man's family
could never be packed up, delivered
to a concentration camp in Idaho.

I say, Minidoka—
what the birds mean is that
there is no such thing
as safety, barely shelter.

minidoka was a concentration camp in idaho

I am afraid that all my ancestors
have gathered my words like birds

collect hair from the dead
for nesting, an abundance of silence,

whole spools of it ready to tether
me to the trees. I am a new father,

too young for ghost stories, too fresh
to remember what it was like to shiver

out on the prairie. I see my own breath,
sometimes when my son cries

at night. He doesn't have to describe
those things he fears in the dark

because my grandmother told me
the world will never be safe for us

when she refused to say the name
of that place we come from. Minidoka,

I say to him and my ancestors lay
fingers across my lips. Do not be ashamed

because we are alive, because the birds
will one day pluck us clean.

american sentences

During World War II, my father was imprisoned in America.

Seattle is far from Michigan, my father from my newborn son.

My father was a child back in that nowhere we call Minidoka.

Minidoka is a Dakota Sioux word meaning "spring of water."

My grandparents were captives too, animals stranded in the badlands.

Some call it relocation, internment; we just call it Idaho.

Before that, they lived in a little house near Seattle's Chinatown.

My Ji-chan worked all day, new gardens sprouting from beneath his huge thumbs.

My Ji-chan worked all night, night watchman pounding a beat through Chinatown.

My Ba-chan went to business college, kept books for Japanese grocers.

My father wasn't yet old enough to understand Minidoka.

Minidoka: family word meaning plume of dust, dirt in our mouths.

When the war broke, the soldiers shipped them all to the Assembly Center.

There, thousands of people waited on their way to the internment camps.

A sad irony: the Assembly Center was called Camp Harmony.

For months, they huddled in chicken coops, wept like piglets, slept like horses.

Camp Harmony was built at what is now the Washington State fairgrounds.

A sad irony: my father took me to the Washington State fair.

We fed the cows, then ate hamburgers on a bench just outside the barn.

He never explained how different the world looks from inside the cage.

Minidoka: that feeling in the animals' guts before slaughter.

When I take my son to the petting zoo, we do not talk about camp.

When I say camp, I mean Minidoka, where we lived without bodies.

I mean Minidoka, where our bodies lived without us inside them.

I was not at Minidoka, but I was bequeathed a piece at birth.

When we say sad irony, we mean Minidoka, still inside us.

I am shingle and tar paper, the sky's dry breath, at Minidoka.

I am barbed wire and fence post and coyote howl, at Minidoka.

I am the crow's bleak song, the National Anthem, at Minidoka.

My son is these things too, or will be when he learns of Minidoka.

After the war, my Ji-chan gave up the garden for a new death grip.

He broke birds by the neck, Minidoka in his hands until he died.

After he died, my Ba-chan lived in the darkest house in the city.

Neither of them ever talked to me about what Minidoka means.

After the war, my father carved out poems about Minidoka.

Poems about the cold desert, about how animals cry at night.

We never talked about what Minidoka means, but we have poems.

My father no longer survives with me on Earth, but we have poems.

Here in Michigan, my son will one day ask what Minidoka means.

One day, we will try to gather what Minidoka means together.

Together, our fingers might not be able to contain all of it.

when we talk about camp

We don't say anything, just hold it in
our mouths like dirty water. We tell stories
to fill the stillness, like that yarn about
the rooster who kills every creature in the forest
so he can weep over the grave of his red hen.
There are songs we sing at funerals that sound
more like animal noises than expressions of grief.
There are words we gulp down like air.

My father makes a pot of coffee in the morning
and explains that the hillside wants to plunge
his house into Puget Sound, confesses
that he does not remember which movies
he has not yet seen. When I look at photos of
my grandfather's shadow, I ask about the snail
shell nailed to the tree in front of the house.
There isn't much to say, he says. It's there.

they say this is how the ogres were invented

My grandfather was not always twisted
by memories of camp. His body
contained so many stories he could not tell
from flesh or marrow. They say this is why
the ogres cry, how the sparrow lost
its tongue in the Idaho scrub.

I once sat at the kitchen table drawing
superheroes—men cloaked in bats, men
with secret powers drawn from the sun.
The only Japanese word I knew
was grandfather. *Ji-chan*, I said—

tell me a story. There are so many
legends about where we come from.
They say this is how the ogres died,
how the witch was bound in barbed wire.

My grandfather told me about that child
sprung from the peach's heart to invade
the ogres' houses for easy plunder.

I put my crayons down and asked
where the ogres lived.

WHERE THE OGRES LIVED

they say this is how fire was invented

This is a poem about where we come from.
It's called *They Say This is How the Crane Wife Fell*.
It's about survival and beast song, concentration
camps, about our ancestors falling
in love. This is a tilt of lightning, they say
through an old man's stomach, a jag
of memory striking down the pear trees
sprouting from his chest. This poem is called

They Say This is How the Moon Remembers Heaven.
They Say This is How the Foxwife Lost Her Brood.
They Say This is How the Witch Burned.

This is an ancient telephone call, the creation
myth of an extinct people. This is a story—
chew it until the words flicker out
on your tongue. This poem is called
They Say This Is How the Ghosts Feel.
It's about not knowing how the ghosts feel.

they say this is how the ogres lived

When the war breaks, you are glad
it's not you exiled to the badlands,
where forest gives way to boneyard.

But then you awaken in that rickety town
assembled by goblins. These are the days
when a man must contain a storm
in his belly, a sad song pressed
tight against his uvula.

These are the years of men squinting
at the weather, at their reflections
fighting for space in broken windows.
These are epochs for beasts prowling
like housecats, dusty paw prints
their only hint of sorrow.

All that remains here are the ribs
left for carnivorous spirits. All that is gone
belongs to the cathedrals of night.

An old man in a cage worries
for the echoes of home, for the fences
that still mark him as sub-human.
He drinks from the bottle, feral now
that he has been tamed. He sits you
on his knee and sings, *boy, let me*
tell you what it means to be a monster.

the ogre's love song

We can be anything—you the huntress,
arrows nocked for game, me
the woodsman keeping the coyotes
at bay. I will carve you a garden

from the brambles, a home
out of those darkest hearts
of wood. You can sing to bluebirds
not cobwebs, to clusters of stars

instead of the gloomy pallor of dusk.
At night, while porcupines sharpen
their bodies against our walls, the elk

their antlers at our door, you can be
a bright song. I will become anything
to protect us from those fiendish shapes
carved for us from the dark.

I will hew an orchard out of the night.
We just have to survive the trees.

they say this is how the ogre lost his heart

Mortality begins with memory
in one hand, inside an egg: that photo
of a bride before the war, that shadow
in the ogre's chest. He reveals
his empty palm, ditched it all
before the pigeons arrived
to roost in his pockets.

A man can fashion a wardrobe of slick
gestures, a legerdemain to keep his house
from caving in, his body from crumpling
into heaps of overcoats. He summons a bouquet
of doves from his hat, a sleeveful of rabbits
quiet and wary for hawks.

Hands can be stealthy, lovesick
foxes or tiny owls who doubt the night.
Memory can be palmed in other locations—
a silent birdcage, a maiden
name, evenings spent sitting
with a vanishing woman.
Try to contain it all in nimble
fingers like miserable yolk.

the ogre's physique

Minidoka is still
a blight on the badlands,
that wreck of stone
where the ogres once wailed
against sinister dust,
harvested pale fruit
from the death orchards.

Here is a root cellar,
now filled with ghosts
of ghosts. Here is a foundation
that might mark the shack
where my grandfather was bent
into awful shapes—wolf-jawed,
lizard-boned, grown to be
food for the centipedes.

This is the pain a man
squeezes into his body
to keep it from his wife
and son. This is the song
he holds in his throat
for decades. Here is a body
shaped like my grandfather's.
Here is my father's body.
Here is my body.

reading comprehension 16: horses' mouths

When the army brought us to the stables on our way to the
concentration camp, they warned us about talking to the
animals. We crowded into the stalls at night and listened to
the horses explain the difference between sugar and glue,
the weight of plow and cart, the jangle of spurs against bare
flank. Their manes sizzled blue, electric as they told us about
Silver riding the Lone Ranger back from the dead, about Man
O' War outracing death. They told us about Comanche, who
survived the Battle of Little Big Horn, who survived America
and we shuddered. Outside, the horses hurtled across the
landscape, from sea to shining shoreline, then back across the
badlands. Pegasus stirred the windstorm with ancient wings.
Sleipnir struck lightning with all eight hooves against the
prairie. Longma broke a cobalt sky with Chinese fire while we
hid our faces under thin blankets. The horses sang low songs
for us, the blues for animals who are more than animals. The
horses used our voices because the words did not fit in their
mouths. When the horses were gone, the trucks took us to
the concentration camp.

Question: What did the horses say?

    a) Horses belong to the world.
    b) There are no horses, just smells of horses.
    c) We should not speak about these things.

the witch's love song

I am not like those pale women
hunted down and drowned
by men who believed too stout
in the Devil's tongue, not
like those crones set ablaze,
mistaken for slaves to their own
carnivorous desire. One day
we will be together in an orchard
near the sea, far from that skeleton
of home we left in the wasteland.
I am not a bird shaped like
a woman, not a woman wielding
fire or broom. You were never
an ogre but a man, his insides
displaced by wasps and the brief
sounds of animals in quicksand.
One day we will be together
again in that brand new house
you will sculpt out of pine trees
and wishbones. Or I will conjure us
a house out of those new words
the spider has invented for love.
We will be together again, once
this body has released its secret
syllables. I can be a woman, you
a man. We will be safe there.

the ogre's love song

It's tomorrow. I've gone
in search of a cow that dissolves,
a carcass drying upside down.
The shank is good for our ancestors—
for so long, I've sought the hungry ones,
the disobedient ones somewhere in Idaho.
Now, the ground transforms into ants
and I wear the desert's tattoo, barbed
wire surrounding invisible places.

Children, silent and transfixed
by pigs' cries, by chickens trapped
in their headless dance—you camouflage
yourselves with feathers and shards
of horn. You live with silverfish,
with potato bugs. Come home.

hogs in the mud, sheep in the sky

It's true—hens do not look at shadows
of foxes, those wicked tangles of sinew
and teeth. They have not considered night
knotted in the predator's beard, dewdrops
sparkling like scalpels. We took what we could
with us to Idaho—dented airplanes,
limbless dolls bundled in tablecloths.

Our families learned to be beasts
at Minidoka, between kitchen and woodshed
where everything collapses into a jangle
of tongue and bone. It's true that we slept
together on stable floors, in chicken houses
dreading the molting season. It's true—

fear permeates the cow's body, despair
a sour taste in the meat. The rooster cries
every morning and the meadow mistakes
his sorrow for the sun.

american children

Never mind the forest's wretched hunger,
those shadows of the witch's hands, those sneaky beasts
cloaked in weeds. Does it matter what befalls

children in the woods? The thrushes will cover them
with stones, will sing about them in some avian
tongue to draw worms closer to the beak.

Hush, now—that cluster of pebbles are unborn
stars wishing themselves skyward. That tangle of moss
shelters promises from the carnivorous night.

The boy will inquire about the distance from willow
to hearth. The girl will wonder about the security
of pigs in their huts, beehives in winter.

Before you blend into the trees, provide them
a dire song about home. Talk about those awful places
so they will know where they are headed.

Explain why the cowbird leaves eggs in
strange nests, how a dwarf spins straw into gold,
then jigs alone in weird stables.

different sorts of trees

We don't sleep anymore, don't even
lie down. Tell me about days before the war,
before you endured Camp Minidoka, whole
bushels of history spilling forth like apples.

       Tell me about your wedding ring, about dancing
       in orchards with my grandfather, about train tracks.

I've lived on the other side of winter, forgot how real
weather feels—the furnace's breath, the showerhead
my only reminder of sky.

       Did he ever gulp whiskey and stumble home
       after dark? Did you ever steal fruit at dawn?

When the ice melts, our house fills with perfume
as the skunks bloom, as pollen swarms venomous
in our night parlor.

       What color were those trees at midnight? Do they
       survive now that you are so far from the farm?
       What about the atom bomb, intoxicating us
       all like orange blossoms now that your husband
       rests in that tiny box of ashes at your bedside?

We can't sleep like horses, don't shed our skins
like leaves, veined, diaphanous in the outlines
of grief. We stand under dark canopies, arms
waving the wind away—we see one another
like we used to, not like we used to.

Now the orchards have all been uprooted, now the orchards stand where they've always been.

reading comprehension 25: children of minidoka

Children of soil play on the back porch as you sleep, their
sleeves drenched in clay. They smell like tombstones for
a hidden epoch, the odor of terrible things happening in
stockyards. Children of wind shimmy over the rooftop, their
shoes all airstream and weathervane. They write their names in
the pine trees and across your shingles, secret names for places
wrapped in barbed wire hidden at the center of a peach. Listen
for children of rain, their murmur in grave tones along gutters
explaining the water cycle, the planetary dance in solar systems,
the rate of a body's decay. This is your house. This is not your
house. Children of flame burn low in the basement where
they hide from me. A sad man with a butcher's knife. A veiled
woman who weeps for lost children.

Question: Where do the ghosts live?

    a) Out on the rings of Saturn.
    b) In tar paper shacks, in chicken coops.
    c) Inside the peach.
    d) All and none of the above.

the witch's love song

A witch blankets herself in whispers
of mysterious pine, studies midnight
with ancient eyes glittering vigilant
from barrow to bough. Some evenings,
unable to sleep, her songs interrogate
the darkness, punctuated with mothlight—
sounds that escape a woman who has lost
her house to war, husband to emphysema.
She might emerge from the gloom
on silent wings, a surge of feathers
and starshine melting swift into wind.
The witch's lips are keen for shrews,
ears sharp for field mice, for taunts
aimed at the dead. When trees break
into a sparkle of lark and cicada,
she will fold herself into a hollow
where she crafts charms against death,
a jagged question about the taste
of birdsong, a new language for grief.

HAUNTINGS

cattle mutilation

In one version of the song, I was born
with a cow's head. We all were
waiting for America to disappear
us from the prairie, tired of scattering
into milk and sirloin across the grass.

In the other version, I am human,
knee-deep in the carrion, fur and gristle
over the nation's bones. I watch people
with blood on their chins. They say God
bless America. They say the animals die,
the animals spring back to life.

remembering minidoka

*And with the camps came extremely significant designations and
distinctions that are with us to this very day: "What camp were
you in?" Or as my great-grandchildren in the next century will
say: "What camp were they in?"*
—*Lawson Fusao Inada,* Legends from Camp

I'm so glad to be at home again!
—*Dorothy Gale,* The Wonderful Wizard of Oz

1.

My grandmother remembered little about Minidoka
because her husband remembered it for them both—
fabricating home from splintered timber
and a lingering taste of horses. She remembered life
before the war—dancing with her husband
in hay-filled barns, fearless walks
across meadow and township, through forests
deep with greedy tigers, through Chinatown.
After the war, she rebuilt her family in that house
brimming with shadows, the forgotten odor
of livestock. After her husband died, she reread
old newspapers in the dim light of her living room,
she gazed at outlines of barbed wire
just beyond her curtains.

2.

My father remembers Minidoka differently—
I remember it all wrong, he says, then explains
how the crows kept him awake, their sorrow

drizzling through morning. When the wolf loped
into camp, my father climbed on its back, rode it
through laundry lines, his fingers digging into fur
reeking of brimstone. He battled hordes of rats
in the hollyhocks, drove them out of gardens
and into fissures beneath other families' barracks.
The memories I have are all that I have,
my father says. They're just memories.
Flocks of sheep devoured hillsides
like earthbound clouds. The hills
caught fire and set the sky ablaze for days.
The children were set to play cat's cradle
only to find they had no thumbs.

3.

When I visited Minidoka, all that remained
was a scar—that debris of family reclaimed
by the earth, that rubble of guard towers,
those broken mousetraps in the remote
curves of the yard. My grandfather's great hands
are buried out somewhere in the thistles.
My father's childhood lies overrun by knotweed
because this is all we have—
the landscape is coated with a black sheen
of memory. The land feels nothing.

dawn's early light

See the night sky detonating in slow motion on the horizon, bleak hills fading into the chatter of birds.

See my son in his bed, his eyes fluttering in dreams, seeing whatever children see moments before they wake.

See my grandmother in 1944, my father about the age my son is now, both of them packed and ready to leave home.

See my grandfather behind them in shadow, his immense hands on their shoulders like he can keep them safe, like he can keep all of us safe.

See those soldiers outside the door, come to take us away to Idaho.

See this memory, the opposite of twilight, this rendering of the world as I understand it, through dream, through conversations with the dead.

See my son eat a waffle for breakfast as the radio gives us the morning news about our own history in America: children stripped from mothers, fathers stripped of their families, all of them stripped of home.

See my son ask for more peaches and be unable to understand any of this.

See me at my father's house about the same age as my son is now; he says this strange word, Minidoka—and I know it's something I don't want to say back to him.

See this word: Minidoka—a beautiful poison, a spider on the tongue, a dry gush of water in the desert of my body.

See our Idaho, a little village of tar-paper roofs and dirt roads surrounded by guard towers and this word Minidoka tangled in the barbed wire.

See my grandparents outside before sunrise because sometimes America is an easier place to live when you can't see it, when it can't see you.

See the first sunrise in Idaho, breath billowing from my grandparents' lungs, from my father's lips in tiny wisps.

See these hands unable to catch that breath—once it dissipates, it's gone.

See these hands unable to catch anything because no one likes to talk about Idaho, about California, about Arizona and Utah and Wyoming—so many points of origin we cannot trace.

See our point of origin, the dark heart, the birth spark, the barrows where our parents once lived in America.

See the prairie illuminated: sunrise and all that's left of our Idaho are the outlines of camp, the silhouettes of our bodies in the dirt.

See me and my son after breakfast: I will have to teach him about Minidoka one day, but this morning he shakes his head, points at the door and says one word—outside.

See the two of us go out, walk through the park across the street and stop near the cemetery on the other side.

See my son pointing back at our house—home, he says and I am happy that he remembers where we came from.

See that sliver of fire at the edge of the universe, Heaven threatening to descend on all our heads.

See this boy with his eyes squeezed tight, his ancestors looking back at him, thirsty for light.

reading comprehension 30: the crane wife

It's never too early to remember she is gone, like that morning the fisherman must cook breakfast for himself—a sliver of eel on a nest of rice. He will wish his plate held something more elegant, like geese cloaked in the rushes or a house full of clean air for clean people. He spent the previous day on the river, casting his net alongside other men in search of fat trout or ingots of gold—something to remind him of how he once lived. He does not remember eyeing seagulls circling overhead, their selfish cries piercing the air like jagged beaks through placid waters. He does not remember the previous week, that loom covered in silk and feathers taunting him until he pitched it into the marsh to be consumed by cattails. It's never too late for old romance, for absent-minded men to capture earthbound birds longing for migration. He will not remember that exchange of talons for sewing needles, that sacrifice of flight for a threadbare mattress. He will pack his suitcase full of filament and bait. He will move to a new village in search of a house where he can forget about thunderstorms, broken wings, and that mysterious young woman with beautiful hands.

Question: What doesn't this fisherman remember?
   a) There are no such things as feathers, only desire for nests.
   b) A windowless room is no substitute for the sky.
   c) There is no such thing as home.

they say this is how the ghosts feel

1.
Minidoka, I never say your name aloud
except when measuring my family's ghosts
against the razor wire still wrapped
around all our tongues.

2.
Minidoka, I cannot contain your name
in my mouth. When I speak it, each syllable
is a storm of crows—feathers, bone, appetite.

3.
There is a flock of dark birds that circle
my house while I sleep. Their jagged song
more death camp than dreamscape, more
car crash than moonrise.

4.
In the dark, my father tries to explain
what Minidoka means. I can almost read his lips
as he releases his lonely howl.

5.
I say your name but it doesn't mean anything
to people whose families were not left wrecked
out on the prairie. So I call you America
and let that name sit on my tongue like dust.

6.
Sometimes, things aren't as terrifying

when they are so far away. I say your name,
America. I say your name, America.
I say your name and wait for you to appear
in my yard—shotgun, noose, barbed wire.

7.
In the dark, my grandfather patrols
up and down city streets, shaking every door
to make sure it's secure. He says America
and then we are all locked out.

8.
America, sometimes, I don't understand
what your name means—four syllables
for home, for not home, for bombs bursting
in air, for believing we are all bombs.

9.
In my dream, my son is learning to talk
but all he says is Minidoka. He is learning
to walk but he just walks in circles.

the wind has always been full of arrows

My grandmother's house once loomed
black against her city block. The war blowing
against staircase and bone, her shrunken body
hidden behind thin windows—bicycles ripping
across her lawn, a dirty game of kickball
threatening the begonias. The neighborhood knew

all about her—that mean Japanese lady, they said.
Tough little witch. When that boy shot her
front door with an arrow, she marched
out to the porch, yanked it free, gnarled fists
daring him to come take it back.

Memory gusts through us, invisible
save for what we see in broken windows—
that prison in Idaho where winter raked
cold teeth across her back, where chicken wire
marked the perimeter of home. There is no place
like a well-disguised scar. I feared my grandmother

when I was a boy, that mildewy perfume of her living
room—at her funeral, my cousin insists she was
the nicest lady in the world. We all agree
that her house didn't stand long enough, its guts
spilling forth a cautious shadow when she finally fell.

year of the monkey

That vanished light is a shadow
where your grandmother once slept.
                    Substitute grief for the monkey.

Her memories of camp Minidoka
are locked away in her house.
                    Substitute sorrow for the monkey.

Substitute sunshine for sorrow
because there is only rain all year long.
                    Subtract a spool of barbed wire

and insert the monkey wherever
you are reminded how long ago
                    your grandmother left camp

and moved her family into a hotel room—
one bed, one window, three bodies all
                    subtracted from the world

and divided by the Idaho plains,
that shadow town where people knew
                    there is no monkey—

only dust and wind and the memory
of how it feels to live in a house.
                    Substitute hope for the monkey

if you dare—new paint for the monkey,
new furniture for the monkey, resurrection
                    for what used to be the monkey.

That new house is another old house
to be emptied and bulldozed one day.
                    Substitute body for house,

for light, for hotel room. Substitute death
for house—the monkey laughs
                    so hard your head pops off.

we sleep like horses

When I dream, I see an open meadow
from my father's living room
windows, the house drained of color
except for the dissolve of night,

a splash of fire, an angel's mane
untamed for the first time
since suffering a gash of spurs.

When my father dreams, he gallops
through the ocean, hooves pounding
the beach like a pair of fists,

his father's fists against that spot
where the moon leaves a zag of sky
on the carpet each evening.

Those things I know in the dark are just
between me and the emptied stables of night,
between me and all those empty houses
I cannot remember while conscious.

When the body is this quiet, the heart may roam
where it desires—so why can't we close
the blinds, relish the darkness? Why can't we
open all our windows so the birds might fly inside?

homeland

Tonight, my father dreams of the land
we all dream of, standing like cattle
on dark plains, hooves planted in the mud,

horns gashing the sky every time we turn
our heads to look at one another. He is dead
and not a hermit crab laying claim

to the shore, not a deer dashing in and out
of shadows as winter looms hungry
over the woods, not a man with his family

still bound to that town made of antlers
and rickety bones. While my father sleeps,
the cattle stampede free of the barbed wire.

This morning, my son ate an orange
segment by segment, his face smeared
with pulp and juice, the peel in shreds

on the kitchen floor. He is alive, unaware
of all the spirits envious of his teeth,
the animals shivering outside. My father

swims away from us, back to the island
where he could put the ocean between us,
whole families of ghosts in the tide.

all the things that make heaven and earth

The soil, the livestock, our memories of the war,
everything flourishing before it vanishes—breath

severed clean from our bodies, our shadows
sunset-deepened and woven with dirt,

whole family trees succumbing to the blight.
My grandfather returns to life, back still

bent by history's quiet yoke, his memories
of camp forever decaying into the tiny garden

behind my house where my father's death
is the soil, where silence blossoms now

all year round. Or the soil is my grandfather
eating darkness, the spectral memory of camp

that feasts upon my father and his father,
me and my son. There are no such things

as ghosts—I tell my son this every evening
as he gazes up the dark stairwell towards his room.

What will be waiting for us when my boy
is old enough to ask where he comes from?

What will we find when our memories of camp
finally molder back into the ground?

ancestral memory

1.

In the evening, my grandfather stands
in the snow outside my bedroom window.
He is barefoot and hungry and as the snow
fills the driveway, as it blankets the yard,
he presses his mouth against the panes
and invites us all outside.

2.

When there is no snow, the yard
is empty, the spirits replaced by tulips.
After midnight, my grandmother in rags
sits on my stomach to remind me how
a thing can remain alive after death.

3.

We believe not in ghosts but in flowers,
in the shape of a blossom that appears
every spring and whispers that word
our family uses in the place of ghosts.

4.

My grandparents are not ghosts—
but that place where they were broken
still lives inside me. There are no ghosts,
only Minidoka, land of woe, a blight
in my body, hereditary decay.

5.

Sing to me a bleak song about Minidoka
and my family. My house is so far away
from Idaho, but so close to the sounds
forest animals make at night. Devour
all the animals, the forest, the song.

6.

This morning, my son's mouth blooms
with milk, white flowers falling over
my shoulder, down my arm to the floor.

twilight's last gleaming

The horses gather in the sky
where the airplanes once were,
flanks radiant in moonlight

as they stamp out places
in the night for our dead to live.

I imagine my grandmother,
a young woman on the prairie
looking up from behind barbed wire

for shooting stars and the horses
rear and whinny like they do at night
when the barn has caught fire
and the doors are locked.

The horses say the night is holy,
each star a socket of light
to remind the earthbound to look away

from the ground. I imagine America
searching the night for airplanes,
for satellites orbiting God and the horses
can't remember when they touched

the Earth last. Perhaps that first dusk
my grandmother watched in Idaho,
the sun's revenant hovering on the hill

before the horses trampled it into soil

for her garden. Or that last sunset
over the water I watched with my father,
ghosts of the plains draping themselves

over our shoulders. The horses just want
to hear us speak our prayers for the dark.

The horses just want to hear us sing.

reading comprehension 44: the hungry ghosts

When the women unfold into gorgeous birds, when the
men peel back their downy pelts, when the children cloak
themselves in hides of long dead antelope—it will be supper
time and your ancestors will emerge from photographs in search
of new clothing. Your grandmother is less a sentimental memory
than a ghost, less a ghost than a woman hungry for peach pie
and the fragile scent of nurseries. Leave a bottle of whiskey in
the yard so she might swallow a quiet fire. Fold the Sunday
paper into a siege of cranes, burn them so she might follow the
smoke home. When a ghoul appears ravenous at your bedside
and looks at you with eyes seething for the tide, she will tell you
about family albums shredded by war, about birds with wings
stripped of plumage, about beasts wailing at the sky to lure
Heaven closer to the trees. She will explain to you what it means
to be caged, will whisper precious between ragged breaths.

Question: What do hungry ghosts whisper?

   a) All the orchards are plagued by hunger.
   b) Tear down the orchards to build houses for ghosts.
   c) There are no such things as ghosts.

ghost story

1.
A child walks through
                  a closed door.

2.
Not a child but everyone
                in my family—
     all walking all the time without seeing
         where we've come from.

3.
     Everyone in my family is dead,
        except for those who are still
alive   amen amen
    to bring the dead back to us.

4.
My grandmother is no longer alive,
        and she tells me stories at night
about Minidoka, about Idaho—
             amen amen

5.
     My grandfather is no longer alive,
and he tells me   stories about my grandmother.
amen amen   They say this is how the lioness
       was turned into a witch. They say
    there is no such thing as magic—
            amen amen

6.

My father is no longer alive,
                and he tells me stories about life
        in a concentration camp.

        They say this is how life is
breathed into a body,   amen amen
        how it feels to be out of breath.

7.

One day the child will grow up and tell me
a story about Idaho, how my family learned
                to pray, how in the end
                no one remembers how to pray.

8.

One day the door will open
                and so many stories spill forth.
They say this is where our hearts are buried.
They say this is how the crows learned our names.
They say Minidoka over and over again
                so that my family can finally sleep.

9.

                There is no child,
        there is no door—
one day my son will ask me
where we come from   amen amen
        and no one will be there
                to tell us the answer.

pilgrims

I hope to take my son one day
to Idaho where our family learned

silence in that ramshackle town
we call Minidoka when no one is listening.

We will look for the outline
of our family's barracks in the dirt—

a line of stones, a strip of rotted wood.
Today, I told a story to my son about that

pilgrimage to Minidoka where the crows
gathered as the names of the dead

were recited, caws and cackles louder
and louder until the last name was uttered—

then morning air, prairie hush. In the night
my son sometimes calls my name

until I go to him, like he is afraid
I will forget where he is. We all have

words we say for unearthly ears—call them
prayers, secrets, vows. Sometimes I say

my father's name in the dark and hope
the birds will sing his name back to me.

american hecatomb

There is another version of the song—
we are all livestock trapped in dark stables.
There is a fire and our bodies wisp
into smoke, a distress signal echoing
for decades after our bones
have been scattered across America.
This never happened but it happens
again every time I close my eyes at night.

My son will ask about that concentration
camp in Idaho one day, about the forgotten
lives of beasts, and I don't yet know
if I want him to recognize his own
carcass back there in the wreckage.

WHERE WE LIVE
NOW

oh, say can you see

America, the place in Seattle where I was
born, where I learned to sing angry songs

for who we are, where we come from. America,
the place in Michigan where my family lives

now in a modest house near a park. I sing this
song along with the radio on my way to work

every morning, along with the jackhammers
breaking the freeway into chunks while I drive.

America, the place in 1942 where my grandparents
once lived—nothing but crows and barbed wire

and shards of us left in the dirt. A concentration
camp in Idaho is a song about how to kill people

without killing them, about those scars striping
a person's insides like tiger skin. America,

the hospital room where my father died in Seattle,
the hospital room in Grand Rapids where my son

was born, and these are both songs about Idaho,
about the world we survived and the world

we must learn to survive. I sing to the birds
at night until they return to the sky

that brought them into this world the way
snow melts to reveal new potholes in the road.

I sing to the ghosts until they recede into hunger
each morning, into the sounds of traffic outside

and all of these songs we sing are America,
heavy and salt-laden in our mouths.

When we sing, we place one hand on our hearts
to make sure it doesn't stop beating.

idaho

Now, imagine your family
hunkered down for winter
in henhouses, in pigpens.
Across the landscape lie

those outlines of rough and
ready warrens, those rubbled
dens for miserable beasts.
In old movies, prisoners carve

hidden tunnels through forests
to Switzerland in black and white.
In ancient tales, hapless peasants
escape dungeons aided by

a crown of bees or feathers
plucked from mystical birds.
This is Camp Minidoka, now
reduced to a sly blemish

on that countryside where
your family imagined escape,
where they were broken in
pieces—one for a shovel, one

for the chickens, the rest scattershot,
broken glass across the prairie.
Strip off your boots, relish each ancient
shard as you hike back to the car.

birthright

Tomorrow, you will ask, where is Minidoka?
I will finish my beer and say nothing
except, it's where you left it.
My father will say Idaho,
but his mother will say, it's right here.

Everyone in our house knows
how easy it is to bring back the dead,
how an answer gnaws its way
through a boy's guts and bursts
from his throat, a wolf's howl,
a carnivorous question

posed to the sky about where we live,
about who else still lives. At night,
I will place my hand on your forehead
and feel the antelope you pursue
with your eyes closed. They are outside
the window now, listening
for your answer.

all of this will be yours one day

My son: I wonder what you will think about
where we come from—that barbed wire

stretching over your head for decades,
those guard towers standing between us

and the prairie yawning all the way to dusk.
The earth desires everything from us, to wrest

ourselves from ourselves, our soft bodies
from our calloused knuckles when all we want

is to stop dreaming that we are animals.
I wonder what you will dream at night

when you learn about Minidoka, about
building a prison with your own hands

then locking yourself away. Years of wartime
hysteria disguised as years of deathly kisses

because somewhere out there on the Idaho
plains lies the foundation of the barracks

my grandfather built to shelter his family
from summer dust, from winter's teeth,

from America. It's easy to build a prison,
easier than to break out of one, at least

when all the locks are fashioned of spirits
and hidden in a man's bones. We still live

in Minidoka's shadows, we who are shadows
of shadows because a desolate landscape

can be sacred without being hallowed and
I wonder what you will build for us.

the origami puzzle

Object: One frog the size of a blackberry
        fashioned from foil, wrapping paper
        from a boy's birthday party. Stroke its back
        and it will leap away.

Inside: Hunger buried in an old man's body
        after his release from camp, a woman's
        skeleton as she twists into knots of ribbon
        and twine—the story etched on all our bones.

Taxidermy: A shooting star, its tail burning shadows
        across the paper. A sparkle of copper burnished
        to gold by a wish. The eye of a puppet.

Geography: You do not need a map to understand
        the terrain. This is a chimney, a root cellar,
        a long winter in the Idaho scrubland. This is a rock
        garden. This is a weed. This is so close to home,
        so far from where we live.

Exhibit A: That ancient table crafted from scrap
        timber after the barracks had been built. Cover it
        with linen in the kitchen. Keep it covered.

Inside: Flip every table to search for names of the dead
        scrawled on the undersides, names of the living
        etched in bone. Where there are knives,
        there are faces waiting to be kissed.

a) You have no idea where that table is now.
b) The last time you carved your name
   into wood, you nearly cut off your thumb.

Geometry: Inside the frog lies a tapestry of angles
           bisected to give the animal its shape, a map
           of the universe creased into planes and pleats,
           a secret to be reassembled by nimble fingers.

Prayer: A collection of scratched records. A broken
        violin. A rusted trumpet, its mouthpiece lost
        to the attic. The shadow of an electric guitar.

Exhibit B: A box of old letters from an old woman
           in Japan, a long-dead aunt who never existed until
           this point, who vanished into a whisper
           when the war split your family like the atom.

Inside: Open those envelopes to see residues of life
        outside Minidoka. Strange characters wriggle,
        spiders scurrying under cabinets and doorjambs
        where they refuse to be deciphered.

c) You never learned Japanese.
d) You are afraid of bugs.
e) Your body is made of bugs.

History: You learned about the atom, never made a bomb.
         You learned about Hiroshima, Nagasaki, about
         Pearl Harbor but never met anyone who was there.

Mythology: Too many frogs expect transformation into
        gorgeous things. At night, they are an orchestra of desire
        trying out different words for family in watery voices.
        By day, they sit at the bottoms of wells and marvel
        at that tiny platform of sky overhead.

Exhibit C: That house on the corner where the witch
        terrorized children for decades, where the shades are
        pulled tight over ancient windows. See how the sky
        blends into shingles. Listen to the water mock
        the sturdiness of gutters.

Inside: Open all the doors to see a tangled human heart.
        Those floorboards know the weight of fear, that staircase
        about that frailty of old women. Free the ghosts
        to explain what they know of imprisonment
        when the walls are unfolded.

Goal: To understand. To never forget about camp.

        f) You were never in camp.
        g) You haven't forgotten.
        h) That place barely exists now on maps.

Biology: Open a frog to see its tiny organs, those ancient
        anatomies hiding beneath skin. Kiss them all
        so they might transform into your ancestors
        with stories about the flimsiness of lily pads.

Genealogy: A pair of forceps, a sledgehammer, and a garden
        trowel left to rust in the dirt. A dust mask. A cowboy hat.
        500 yards of barbed wire, a coal stove and a bare light bulb.

A transistor radio. A roll of toilet paper. A jug of whiskey.
A fly-swatter. A dog-eared Bible, a scalpel and
a torn map of the United States. A suitcase.

Instructions: Unfold everything with steady hands,
cautious where paper is thin at the seams. Take it
apart, press it flat against the table and ignore
those wrinkles that used to hold the body
together. What do you make of this?

reading comprehension 53: the peach boy

Every entrance is an exit, but when that woman discovers an infant in a strange piece of fruit, she does not wonder about rumpled bits of blanket left in distant cribs, a hollow throat choking as boughs once laden with blossoms are reduced to kindling. Every exit is a spark, so when a magical boy strikes out to fetch rubies from faraway lands, his mother will smolder for years in the peach groves. He might wage war on witches and ogres, gather their babies and pitch them all into the bonfire. He might challenge the atom bomb to a contest of illumination. Every spark is a hope for flame, so when that boy fails to return home, the orchards will be bursting with new creatures: burned monkeys, wingless pheasants, dogs who sing sad songs in hoarse voices. Explain to that woman how her children are a bestiary for someone else's story, how mooncalves emerge squirming in edible places. Hope is a stone forsaken by long-extinct flora—it lies heavy as coal in the palm, delicate as an infant's skull. Watch her plant it in dry soil and linger to see what might sprout.

Question: What is hope?

a) A jewel for the blind.
b) A pomegranate full of healthy animals.
c) A tiny shrine for the abandoned.
d) Nothing.

love song

There are no such things as ghosts—
just this flurry of dust, a burst of feathers
too easily mistaken for witches
hungry for reverence and blood oranges.
Those ogre bones lurking in mirrors
will try to eat your reflection. Those teeth
hanging vicious from the eaves are homeless
rivers reaching for the ground.

When I die, let me return as moths
in your overcoat, as that scrape of crows
circling your chimney, as a plume
of your breath dangling
in the breeze like a wish.

fish are jumping

The fish in the river are all beautiful
fish, obsidian-scaled trout, koi
with the evil eye, salmon with shiny tongues.

I am not singing about fish,
but about your ancestors
who once lived in the land of the dead.

Call the trout grandfather
and he will carry you downstream
on his back. Call the koi grandmother
so she will use her magic to protect you
in the overcrowded waters.

Call the salmon uncle and auntie—
they will swallow you in pieces
to keep you safe.

There is a place on the river
where the fish jump straight into
the fishermen's nets because there is
no river, just fish squirming together,
a volt of fins and scales in the dirt.

Go to sleep now, and one of these
mornings, you will ask me how high
a fish can jump out of the water.

I'll say there are no fish. I'll say
there is no such thing as jumping.

when i ask my son to speak

1.
He refuses tonight, but my father begins,
my grandfather grumbling in the beyond.

2.
He opens his mouth and my grandmother
tells a story about the ocean battering itself
against the stones beneath my father's house.

3.
He says nothing. I have not been to Minidoka,
never slept in a hungry yard, never stood
behind barbed wire to watch the Idaho sky
darken like a wish fulfilled.

4.
He says nothing—pine trees fill with sparrows,
then sag under several months' snow.

5.
Men sliced into angry fish, women withered
to lacquered bones—he says nothing of this.

6.
One day, all our mouths will be open, voices
pouring into other voices, cresting at night.

7.
He hasn't yet learned to speak.
No one has taught us what words mean.

they say this is how the bone sings

The Nisei told their children, "Don't make waves. Don't stand out.
You are different enough anyway."
> —*Personal Justice Denied, Report of the Commission on*
> *Wartime Relocation and Internment of Civilians*

There is a place along the border
where children sleep in the dark
like there was once a prairie in Idaho
where my father learned what Minidoka means—
a concentration camp under that scar
spangled sky, all our ancestors bound
in razor wire and splintered wood,
the moon's careless gaze over all of us.

There is a place where the boys are still
wrestling wild boars bare-fisted, where
girls are murdered gathering jonquils
in dry meadows. Listen—the night is filled
with the owls' grief for tiny bodies
concealed in unimaginable places.

There is a story about a woodsman who ate
meat without bones for weeks without
ever wondering where his children were.
Before I die, let all the children carve
a flight of flutes from my ribcage,
a symphony revealing every wound
on our fathers' bodies, a song
proclaiming we will never be dead.

they say this is how the heart works

Today, Japanese Americans are not often viewed as unassimilable
aliens; since the racial turmoil of the 1960's, indeed, they have been
portrayed as the "model minority," a group with high educational
and professional achievements, model citizens free of most social
pathology who do not agitate or disturb the status quo.
　　　　—Personal Justice Denied, Report of the Commission on
　　　　Wartime Relocation and Internment of Civilians

Quiet and furious labor—they say
this is how the heart works
to safeguard a home. Sanctuary
or confinement—they say this
body aches for transformation
into beasts who refuse to be eaten.

Men have locked their bones in
upright configurations, patient now
for new trees. Women have grown
accustomed to beautiful hair, long
for fresh plumage to set the backwoods
ablaze. The cranes steer clear of me
afraid of fingers that tear tailfeathers
from fragile forms, in fear of fishermen
who shear wings from seabirds.

They say this is how my grandfather
lost his tail, how my grandmother lost
her will to sail over seascapes.
Furious shame, goddamn moon—

this is how my body wants to curdle
something sweet, how my skeleton aches
to be filed into points. This is how
my teeth chew my name.

loyalty questionnaire

1. How do you pronounce your real name?

2. How do you pronounce your identification number in your native tongue?

3. Is the mouse more loyal to the cat or to the cheese? What does this say about the mousetrap?

4. Do you look more like your mother or the President of your country?

5. What noises do they make to celebrate the country where you were born? When the neighborhood dogs howl at night, do you sing along?

6. You have lived inside a closed box for three years. What grateful words will you say to your captors when they finally lift the lid to set you free?

7. When you pray, what does God look like when you open your eyes?

8. Recite the Pledge of Allegiance, but sing it to the tune of a song that is popular for dancing in your country. Don't you think that is disrespectful?

9. How do you feel about your country? Choose from the following:

    a) Does the scarecrow do the crops' bidding?
    b) Does the machete sharpen itself against bone?
    c) When do Halloween masks go on sale?

10. You are walking in the city and discover a young man unconscious on the sidewalk. He has no identification so you take twenty dollars from his wallet and leave.

11. Is the sword loyal to the hand? Is the tongue loyal to the mouth? What are you thinking about when you cover your mouth with your hands?

12. How many horses have you ridden in your life? What were their names? Where do they live now?

13. In your country, there is an abandoned zoo where the animals wait in their cages for someone to rescue them. There is a party just outside the zoo, everyone high on sugar and fireworks. What will you do with that gun hidden under your jacket?

14. Recite the Pledge of Allegiance, but do it in that mocking tone your father uses when he talks about America.

15. There is a stable with a leaky roof. The animals are trapped together standing belly-deep in rainwater, their cries inaudible out there on the prairie. What can you think of that is sadder than this?

16. Describe it using only questions you wish you had asked your grandmother before she died.

17. Do the bees pledge loyalty to the hive? What is honey in the land of the dead?

18. What is night in your country? A place for the constellations to reenact the wars we make on Earth? A black eagle hunting animals in the dark? A haven for ghosts?

19. There are no such things as ghosts except for your ancestors' shadows crouching at the foot of your bed while you sleep. How

does your name taste in the mouths of the dead?

20. Recite the Pledge of Allegiance, but replace the words with black seawater, with huge gulps of brine and the sounds a boat makes as it splinters against the rocks.

21. What are your least favorite animals to eat in your country? In your house?

22. Are you loyal to your animals? What animals would you kill to defend your country?

23. Why do you keep hearing the word *animals* when I am clearly saying *children*?

24. How does the moth's body come to be filled with dust? Can you say the word *moon* without thinking of the moon? What kind of animal is inside your body?

25. You overhear a foreign woman on her cell phone. You can't understand her, but her words sound filthy and mangled. What language do you think she is speaking?

26. What do you think she is saying about your country?

27. Is the rain loyal to the clouds? Are fish loyal to the ocean? If you could live anywhere in the world, where in America would you live?

28. Do you renounce loyalty to those foreign governments you serve, your treacherous herds, your covens?

29. When you return from the war, your house will be empty. Who remembers how to cook your favorite meal? Or do the horses gather in your room at night to graze on your silence?

30. Recite the Pledge of Allegiance, but replace the words with the names of all the ancestors you have forsaken.

31. Recite your ancestors' names, but replace their names with blood.

32. If you could die anywhere in the world, where would you bleed?

33. When you are bleeding, can you recite your name over and over again until it becomes the Pledge of Allegiance? What color is your blood then?

legacies of camp

1.
The first rule in talking about camp is
we do not talk about camp.

2.
Minidoka is a word we use for camp.
Relocation is a fancy way of talking
about internment, camp a polite
word for prison. Minidoka.

3.
The cage is the skeleton for grief, grief
the mantle worn by shame, shame the fuel
for a tone-deaf heart.

4.
They say this is where the witch burned,
where the ogre lost his heart. Sing a real song
for imaginary creatures. Keep it simple
so the ghosts can sing along.

5.
Men bruised by sticks.
Men pummeled by stones.
Men disintegrated by wind.
Men gashed to pieces by wild animals.
Men shredded by flights of dark birds.
Men evaporating into morning.

6.

What turns kings into beasts, princesses
into crones hungry for dusk? How do we lose
our ancestors still living in barren houses
next door? What do horses dream about,
buttressed by the rigor mortis of night?
Remember: we do not talk about camp.

7.

The second rule: there are no trick questions,
only bear traps poised silent in hope
that someone will talk about camp.

8.

The cage houses the heart of the ogre,
the ogre the glamor bewitching
the wilderness. We live at the fringe
of awful desire, that ragged edge of twilight
where the ocean devours the shore.
Remember the cage.

9.

They say those ruins are nearly swallowed
by the Idaho scrubland. I've seen ruins
posing as old men on bar stools, women
cloaked in thorns and sharks' teeth.
We do not talk about ruins.

10.

Men who smoke in restaurants.
Men who try to quit smoking.
Men who try to quit smoking for their children.

Men who smoke only when drinking.
Men who smoke in cars with the windows up.
Men who smoke in secret places.
Men who never knew they were on fire.

11.
The cage shelters us from despair, despair
the ocean lapping at our knees, fear the eels
wriggling electric on the incoming tide.
The cage holds everything we do not talk about.

12.
Third rule: Do not speak—listen to buzzards
pasted against every sunset, to alley cats
yowling lonesome in the glow of night.
That is a soliloquy of ruin. This is
the hush of mushrooms on fallen trees.

13.
Stories are tiny prisons built to house
our secrets. We live in cages still.
My grandmother's legs remain bound
by barbed wire. My grandfather's tongue
lay caked in dust. Everyone is dead.
It was goddamn camp—we can't talk about it.

looking outside airplane windows

I expect to see that boy
in the clouds, sad faced,
barbed wire tattoo ablaze
where no one can see it—

not a tattoo but a scar wrapped
around his belly like a belt
cinched tight to hold his body

together. Every cloud dissolves
one day, leaving so many boys
in the sky, hanging, waiting to fall
back to Earth. Girls too, hearts

where their stomachs should be,
guts twisted into brambles
now for the body's deep sorrow
because we have so many words
for clouds: father, grandfather,

and one day, son. We spend our lives
searching for your shapes.

You already resemble those shapes
we know by heart.

rocket's red glare

My favorite thing is space, stars shivering
as the darkness gathers in silent plumes

over our heads. Tonight, my father ignites
the sky to let us know where we are

all headed one day—we live together
on the ground, whether or not we like it

when the landscape is littered with dead birds,
with beautiful carcasses that can't recall

how it feels to be close to Heaven. Tonight,
there are other things in the sky, and a poem

is a thing I make in the dark as my son plays
at sleeping, while he dreams of jumping

on the moon, so far from where we live
in America. Once we lived in a concentration

camp in Idaho, a distant memory when it was
a fire in my father's chest, more distant

now that it burns in mine. Once, we sang
like wolves out in the snow, faces

turned up at the constellations and hoping
someone out there understands and howls back

and God, that great silence reverberates
through all of us. Tonight, my father sings

no longer, but where there is fire, there is fire.
The heat is my father's. The smoke is mine.

And when my son looks up at the sky,
he will notice how small everything looks

from far away—a bomb is a flicker of light,
then a flurry of dust, then darkness.

NOTES

Personal Justice Denied is a report prepared by the Commission on Wartime Relocation and Internment of Civilians. This official government study of the internment of Japanese Americans during World War II, as well as the effects of the war on Alaskan natives in the Pribilof and Aleutian Islands, was ordered by the U.S. Congress in 1980; it concluded that Executive Order 9066, which made possible the relocation and incarceration of approximately 112,000 people of Japanese ancestry in the United States, was fueled by "race prejudice, war hysteria, and a failure of political leadership" rather than any kind of military need.

The American Sentence is a form invented by Allen Ginsburg: one sentence in seventeen syllables with a reference to a location—his attempt to Americanize the Japanese Haiku form.

The Reading Comprehension poems are inspired by the Haibun, a Japanese form that consists of a passage of prose followed by a Haiku.

"They Say This Is How Fire Invented" is after "Immigrant Blues" by Li-Young Lee. "When I Ask My Son to Speak" is after "I Ask My Mother to Sing," also by Li-Young Lee.

The questions in "Loyalty Questionnaire" are inspired by *The Book of Questions* by Pablo Neruda, by the poem "Famous" by Naomi Shihab Nye, by the Voigt-Kampff Test used to reveal whether a person is a human or replicant in the movie *Blade Runner*, and by Selective Service Form 304A, the "Loyalty Questionnaire" given to adults incarcerated at Minidoka and other concentration camps in the United States during World

War II. This questionnaire was administered and then scored to determine a person's loyalty by way of how "American" their answers were.

More information about the incarceration of Japanese Americans during World War II can be found online at many places, including Densho (densho.org), the *Japanese American Exhibit & Access Project* on the University of Washington Libraries website, and in *Personal Justice Denied*, the full text of which is available at the U.S. National Archives and Records Administration website.

ACKNOWLEDGEMENTS

Thank you to all the editors who have worked on the following anthologies and journals in which these poems have appeared, sometimes in different forms.

Alaska Quarterly Review: "Homeland" and "They Say This Is How the Ghosts Feel"

Asian-American Literary Review: "American Children" and "The Origami Puzzle"

The Bakery: "They Say This Is How the Ogre Lost His Heart" and "They Say This Is How the Ogres Lived"

The Big Scream: "Birthright," "Reading Comprehension 25: Children of Minidoka," "They Say This Is How the Ogres Were Invented," and "The Ogre's Love Song [It's tomorrow. I've gone]"

Baltimore Review: "Reading Comprehension 30: The Crane Wife" and "Reading Comprehension 53: The Peach Boy"

Bellingham Review: "Legacies of Camp"

The Cortland Review: "Oh, Say Can You See" and "Dawn's Early Light"

Construction: "They Say This Is How the Bone Sings"

Cotton Xenomorph: "Pilgrims"

DIAGRAM: "American Sentences," "Ghost Story," "Loyalty Questionnaire," and "Twilight's Last Gleaming"

Fifth Wednesday: "When We Talk About Camp"

The Fourth River: "American Hecatomb," "Ancestral Memory," "Cattle Mutilation," "Fish Are Jumping," and "Year of the Monkey"

Hawai'i Review: "All of This Will Be Yours One Day" and "When I Ask My Son to Speak"

Heavy Feather Review: "Rocket's Red Glare"

Hunger Mountain: "Looking Out Airplane Windows," "Reading Comprehension 16: Horses' Mouths," and "All the Things That Make Heaven and Earth"

Jet Fuel Review: "The Wind Has Always Been Full of Arrows" and "The Witch's Love Song [A witch blankets herself in whispers]"

Kartika Review: "They Say This Is How the Heart Works"

Lantern Review: "The Birds Know What They Mean"

Los Angeles Review: "Remembering Minidoka"

Massachusetts Review: "Minidoka was a Concentration Camp in Idaho"

Skidrow Penthouse: "Hogs in the Mud, Sheep in the Sky"

Song of the Owashtanong: Grand Rapids Poetry in the 21st Century: "Different Sorts of Trees" and "We Sleep Like Horses"

Sweet: A Literary Confection: "Different Sorts of Trees" and "We Sleep Like Horses"

TRNSFR: "Idaho"

Weave: "Love Song"

Word Riot: "Reading Comprehension 44: The Hungry Ghosts"

Thank you to my family, immediate and extended, who live with internment in their histories. In particular, thank you to my late father, Lonny Kaneko, and my late grandparents, Lois Kaneko and Sanetomo Kaneko.

There are so many who have supported me directly and indirectly in my writing of these poems. Thank you to my Poets Choice crew, past and present: Amorak Huey, Chris Haven, Amy McInnis, Aaron Brossiet, Ashley Cardona, Katie Cappello, Brian Clements, Brian Komei Dempster, Judy Halebsky, Christina Olson, Jean Prokott, Dean Rader, and Mark Schaub. Thank you to Matthew Gavin Frank and Douglas S. Jones, who read this manuscript in an earlier form. Thank you to my friends and colleagues in the Writing Department at Grand Valley State University. Thank you to the *Waxwing* team. Thank you to Kundiman fellows, faculty, and staff everywhere.

Thank you to Diane Goettel and the staff at Black Lawrence Press for believing in this book.

Thank you to my son Leo for shifting how I understand the world in the most important way, and thank you to Caitlin Horrocks for putting up with me and supporting me through the writing of these poems. You are the best people I have ever met.

www.ingramcontent.com/pod-product-compliance
Lightning Source LLC
Chambersburg PA
CBHW031931090426
42811CB00002B/151